Keys to Mental Freedom!
By: Pastor Danaz Williams

Graphic Cover design by Antonio Curry
Editors: Nicosia Bennett and Markette Williams

Printed in the United States of America
First Printing Edition, 2024

ISBN 978-1-7361577-9-4

V&G Publishing LLC
Nottingham, MD 21236

My Inner Peace is consistent with the inner I AM!

ACKNOWLEDGEMENTS

I thank God for being born and being graced with the ability to give His truth in order to help all find inner peace. I give love to all my family members and friends.

Table of Contents

Purpose

This is a gift of freedom to free individuals' minds from fear, defeat, and devastation! I once was afraid of my "I AM greatness," until I understood the power of liberty, which is freedom!

"I AM whatever you say I am and if I wasn't then why would I say I am!" - Marshall Mathers

I am a product of MiLiFe. Let "Peace" begin!

Introduction

I introduce to you, yourself. You are who you say you are. This freedom guide to peace is a spiritual guidance and guideline to one's happiness. This is a PURSUIT!

You have to experience all spiritual situations in life before you rest eternally. We want to believe this is a natural experience that we have come to experience in this day and age, however, I beg to differ. It's a spiritual experience and journey; be it good, bad, and/or indifferent.

You! You are the key to mental freedom for yourself. Are you ready to take this leap of healing? If you are, let's go!

Chapter 1
I Am Joy!

Joy, I am joy! Regardless of my struggles, I will have it. I will no longer stay in an unjoyful space or situation! I will no longer settle for what is natural joy, but I'm striving for spiritual joy!

Webster describes joy as, "the emotion evoked by well-being, success, or good fortune or by the prospect of possessing what one desires."

I AM describes joy as, "You make known to me the path of life; in your presence, there is fullness of joy; at your right hand are pleasures forevermore." Psalm 16:11

The Quran
Whosoever does right, whether male or female, and is a believer, we shall make them live a good life, and We shall pay them a recompense in proportion to the best of what they used to do. (16: 97)

Buddhism

Life, though full of woe, holds also sources of happiness and joy, unknown to most. Let us teach people to seek and to find real joy within themselves and to rejoice with the joy of others! Let us teach them to unfold their joy to ever-sublimer heights! Noble and sublime joy is not foreign to the Teaching of the Enlightened One. Wrongly, the Buddha's Teaching is sometimes considered to be a doctrine diffusing melancholy. Far from it: the Dhamma leads step by step to an ever purer and loftier happiness. -Nyanaponika Thera (1901–1994)

What is God-given is called nature; to follow nature is called Tao (the Way); to cultivate the way is called culture. Before joy, anger, sadness, and happiness are expressed, they are called the inner self; when they are expressed to the proper degree, they are called harmony. The inner self is the correct foundation of the world, and the harmony is the illustrious Way. When a man has achieved the inner self and harmony, the heaven and earth are orderly, and the myriad of things are nourished and grow thereby. - Confucius

What is the "I AM" saying in me? In order to fulfill joy, we must come together and allow our spiritual being to accept this form of happiness!

Chapter 2
I Am Peace!

Peace! What is it? Some may say, "a two-finger salute," others may say a space that has me in a great place. I'm at peace!

I AM at peace! Peace is the gift that is established through the I AM in you to be.

What do you want to be? If you want it, you can attain it! You have to let go and believe in your spiritual connection to peace to fulfill this peaceful journey. The I AM is going to be in peace. The I AM is the true fulfillment of the spiritual world for all of us to have peaceful thinking, peaceful space, and a peaceful life. It is yours!

"And a harvest of righteousness is sown in peace by those who make peace."
James 3:18

The I AM in you made this attainable, you just have to believe that you can attain it.

"If possible, so far as it depends on you, live peaceably with all."
Romans 12:18

It depends on us! I'm willing and I'm more than capable of being at peace.

To my Jewish brothers and sisters, the I AM in me greets you, "Shalom" (peace) is one of the underlying principles of the Torah.

Proverbs 3:17 "Her ways are pleasant ways and all her paths are shalom (peace)."

We must walk together to create this peaceful space!

To my Islamic brothers and sisters, "salaam" (سلام) (peace). I salute you in my I AM space loving you as my neighbor!

I want freedom for all spiritually!
To my Hindu family, "Shanti" (शांति)!

This space will be created!

To my Buddhist family "Namo!" This is what I greet you with.

It's a must that the I AM in me builds this space for all mankind!

Proverbs 3:5-6: This is MiLife!

"Peace to all and to all a peaceful life!"

Chapter 3
I Am Love!

Wow! This word is a word that brings so much joy and so much pain. Love is truly an action that many can't comprehend.

1 Corinthians 13:4-5, "Love is patient, love is kind. It does not envy, it does not boast, it is not proud. It does not dishonor others, it is not self-seeking, it is not easily angered, it keeps no record of wrongs," In order to begin to comprehend love you first have to love yourself.

What do you mean? The I AM in me loves me. So much so, that I've become clear on my assignment to love! It's an unconditional assignment for me! Notice I didn't say "commitment," I said assignment. I've been assigned by the I AM in me to love because the I AM first loved me and is still loving me. This is not a choice. I have accepted this thought of action for and from the spirit to be able to remove any type of pain. So much so, that I walk in the joy of love because the I AM in me has made that decision.

Healing through the process of love is self-fulfilling. It's an inner peace that you have to be willing to accept for yourself!

So many are afraid to express and accept love; especially if their cultural or religious beliefs want them to believe differently. Healing within is a part of your inner self to love yourself unconditionally and/or your neighbor! This is how the world will heal!

Understanding my Jewish brother, being at peace with my Arabic brother, sitting down with my Indian brother, and hearing others and understanding their beliefs will change the course of the non-loving relationships in this world!

When the I AM speaks of love; what is expressed?

John 15:12 KJV
"This is my commandment, That ye love one another, as I have loved you."

One another! The one another doesn't have a religious title to who's the one, it's everybody! That's the importance of love.

I want to see healing and I know understanding is the key! So understanding the structure of love through other religious beliefs can give the unknown an idea and some insight into the spiritual nature of others.

There are two main Arabic words which have been used in the Quran for love. One of them is ḥubb (حبّ) and its derivatives and the other is mawaddah (مودّة).
Mawaddah is love that is expressed in actions. However, ḥubb and maḥabbah (محبة) refer to a state of the heart.

Once again, it's an individual's understanding of where they choose to be; a state of the heart.

Love through the Torah. Love among human beings.

One of the core commandments of Judaism is "Love your neighbor as yourself." (Leviticus 19:18)

"If you look into your own heart, and you find nothing wrong there, what is there to worry about? What is there to fear?"
- Confucius

"Attack the evil that is within yourself, rather than attacking the evil that is in others." - Confucius

We have to be clear on one thing, it's the individual and what they want to be healed from.

Love, simply put in this Buddhist definition, is "unselfishly wishing others to be happy; to be delighted to be in their presence; to offer our affection and smiles and hugs and help freely without wanting anything in return."

I want healing for all humanity:

- That we will live in harmony.
- That we will gain understanding through love and show this action to fulfill the purpose of unity.

Chapter 4
I Am Happiness!

The thought of happiness is the fulfillment of one's self-understanding. I am happy! I am happy! I am happy! I stand in the spiritual direction and presence of happiness! Note, not because I'm happy but because I AM is happy. What do I mean? It is a consistent work. It's not based on my day; it's based on my servitude. The I AM is happy because I understand my purpose to serve. **We have to remove the stigma of being a servant, and "not a slave"!** It's a gift that allows you to be happy and or the happiest in your space in life. I am happy with my days work!

Many leaders may speak on happiness, especially for mental health. However, until you allow the I AM in you to direct your path, you will struggle to achieve happiness. It's a removal of one's self and a transition into one's spirit. I am happy!

Falah (happiness) gives sustainable peace and tranquility as explained in the Quran AlYKahf 46: "Wealth and sons are allurement of the life of this world; but the things that endure, good deeds, are best in the sight of thy Lord, as rewards, and best as (the foundation for) hopes."

Happiness is very much sustainable when you trust your spiritual assignment.

"If you want others to be happy, practice compassion. If you want to be happy, practice compassion." - Dalai Lama

"All that we are is the result of what we have thought. It is founded on our thoughts. It is made up of our thoughts. If one speaks or acts with an evil thought, pain follows one, as the wheel follows the foot of the ox that draws the wagon. All that we are is the result of what we have thought. It is founded on our thoughts. It is made up of our thoughts. If one speaks or acts with a pure thought, happiness follows one, like a shadow that never leaves."

I AM doesn't want your happiness to go anywhere. It's a great space that is consistent with your everyday journey.

The Torah touches on five simple rules for happiness.

Five Simple Rules for Happiness

1. Free your heart from hatred.
(Leviticus 19:17)

2. Free your mind from worries.
(Talmud Yevamot 63b)

3. Live simply.
(Psalms 116:6)

4. Give more.
(Deuteronomy 15:11)

5. Expect less.
(Jeremiah 4:5)

We are so afraid to understand that the more we learn the more we gain clarity.

I'm clear on one thing, the I AM in me is happy.

Chapter 5
I Am Success!

I wanted to understand the spiritual aspect of success! This is a mental destroyer! The basis of the word and how it is proclaimed with so much importance can cause individuals to go insane. I remember when I was driven by success and not knowing that the I AM in me was already successful. I couldn't fill that space in my life because I was unable to reach the quote-on-quote level of success that I should have or had obtained. However, spiritually I was successful and didn't even know. Simply put, I was alive! The I AM in me allowed me to live! We have to tell ourselves, *my life is a success just because I was born and I AM alive!*

We are a group of individuals seeking a balance that is consistent with a successful life. Our lives become more successful once we are willing to understand each other in our own spiritual space in this world. That's why these black words on this white paper are so meaningful because it's not successful without them coming together.

The I AM in me wants to understand the spirit that drives your success, your joy, your peace, your love, and your happiness! This is a healing call for a spiritual awakening that will stop dividing and subtracting the people, but will multiply and add growth to our success to acknowledge the oneness of humanity. Simply put, we are all human and we should be one successful race!

Successful in the Bible reads.
"And be not conformed to this world: but be ye transformed by the renewing of your mind, that ye may prove what is that good, and acceptable, and perfect, will of God." Romans 12:2 KJV

The world wants us to be conformed to separation and that's not a successful lifestyle. We can still be structured by our own cultural beliefs and live in harmony with our neighbors. We choose to not be successful in that area of life. We want to label, to divide, and that's not beneficial to one's growth as one's harmony.

"Success depends upon previous preparation, and without such preparation, there is sure to be failure."
- Confucius

The I AM in me is prepping me through knowledge to understand your beliefs and your culture. Preparing me to be successful when I'm in your presence.

The I AM didn't come to offend. I came to understand my neighbor so we can be successful in the same community of life!

"They are one (true) guidance from their Lord, and they are the successful."
(Al-Baqara, Chapter 2, Verse 5)

We have a spiritual guidance. The more we truly study and are willing to understand our brothers and sisters, the more we will all be the successors of the mental peace of being successful.

I Am Success!

Chapter 6
I Am Unstoppable!

I am and I will not be stopped until I am called home to rest by my Lord and Savior Jesus, the Christ.

The I AM in me has challenged me to press towards the mark of the high calling. The I AM is coming to unite all brothers and sisters in unity with the spirit of belief.

I am personally not questioning one's beliefs. I am here to serve in unity of a global movement that will create mental peace and prosperity for all nations.

This is the will of God and it's unstoppable! We can't let differences (in)beliefs and religions stop us from becoming a united force.

If you notice, all leaders were assassinated for trying to build this unity because it defies the structure of the culture of the world.

The more I'm separated from something, the less I know of it! The less I know of it the less I want it to be around. The less that it's around me, the less I care for it! The less I care for it, the less it concerns me! The less it concerns me, the less I think about it! The less I think about it, it's not on my mind! The less it is on my mind, I then forget about it! The more I forget about it, it has now become lost.

I can't lose my understanding and my concern for others. The I AM didn't, and **He** died for humanity. The I AM in me wants me to die to self for the servitude of others. This is an unstoppable movement that will cause unity and mental peace for all nations.

If I present myself as an understanding vessel to my brothers and sisters who believe in Hinduism, Judaism, Christianity, Buddhism, Islam, Sikhism,

Jainism, Bahá'í Faith, Zoroastrianism, Taoism, Confucianism, Anglicanism, Rastafari, Mandaeism, Bábism, Wicca, Lutheranism, Tenrikyo, Catholicism, Methodism, Benzhuism, Pentecostalism, and Adventism, we then gain understanding and become unstoppable together; bringing peace to the world and creating a peace of mind.

It's so important to be unstoppable in your beliefs to bring peace of mind to all humanity! We deserve to be at peace. There's enough war going on in our own spaces in our minds to keep battling with one another. It's time for a peaceful peace of mind. Furthermore, the more we understand one another the more unstoppable we will be. The I AM in me will not stop until I see a global peace of mind.

Chapter 7
I Am Capable!

This is where, through all life struggles, you release. Regardless of what's been said to you, the I AM in you and I, is capable!

We believe in Philippians 4:13
"I can do all this through him who gives me strength. This means I'm more than capable."

Don't settle! Furthermore, become more than what it looks like compared to what the situation may be! This is how you create your peace and your inner understanding of what your destiny in life is.

You are more than capable to have:
I am Joy!
I am Peace!
I am Love!
I am Happiness!
I am Success!

This is unstoppable if you believe in your spiritual connection to what will establish your understanding to a healthy healing lifestyle. Speak these things into existence!

"And never say 'I will definitely do this tomorrow' without adding if God wills. But if you forget, then remember your Lord and say, 'I trust my Lord will guide me to what is more right than this." Quran 18:23-24

We are more than capable.

"With realization of one's own potential and self-confidence in one's ability, one can build a better world."
Dalai Lama XIV

This is being capable of understanding where my brothers and sisters may stand on their beliefs when it comes to a healthy lifestyle.

"To be able, under all circumstances, to practice five things constitutes perfect virtue; these five things are gravity, generosity of soul, sincerity, earnestness, and kindness." - Confucius

Enlightenment is key
Top 10 Buddha Quotes

"Do not dwell in the past, do not dream of the future, concentrate the mind on the present moment."

"It is better to conquer yourself than to win a thousand battles. Then the victory is yours. It cannot be taken from you, not by angels or by demons, heaven or hell."

"It is better to travel well than to arrive."

"Peace comes from within. Do not seek it without."

"The only real failure in life is not to be true to the best one knows."

"The way is not in the sky. The way is in the heart."

"There is nothing more dreadful than the habit of doubt. Doubt separates people. It

is a poison that disintegrates friendships and breaks up pleasant relations. It is a thorn that irritates and hurts; it is a sword that kills."

"Thousands of candles can be lighted from a single candle, and the life of the candle will not be shortened. Happiness never decreases by being shared."

"We are what we think. All that we are arises with our thoughts. With our thoughts, we make the world."

"What we think, we become."

This is number eleven and this jumped off the page for me! The I AM in me can agree.

"However, many holy words you read, however many you speak, what good will they do you if you do not act on upon them?" — Buddha

I am capable of unity, great health, and truth! The truth is I AM wants me to love my neighbor as I love myself. The spirit also wants me to do unto others as I would do unto myself.

I am more than capable of understanding my journey with my Lord and Savior Jesus, the Christ. It has brought me peace. Even more, I have accepted the calling of the Great I AM to share the light and love of unity with all humanity! I am more than capable.

Chapter 8
Conclusion

We are so afraid of the truth! We have been placed against each other by this so-called structure of life. We can no longer stand by allowing truth to not be the full motivation of our existence. Why? Because, until we as a world accept the truth we will be bound to the lies of its structure.

There are many points on truth!

John 8:32
 "And you will know the truth, and the truth will set you free."

What do we need to be free from, all this self-inner nonsense known as "SIN"?

I've created a space so it must be true! Yes, it may be true to you but is it truth?

1 John 3:18

"Little children, let us not love in word or talk but in deed and in truth."

Can I be truthful to what I believe to be true, "the more we are truthful to ourselves the more we will be free of life."

"'This is the Day when the truthful will benefit from their truthfulness.' For them are gardens [in Paradise] beneath which rivers flow, wherein they will abide forever, Allah being pleased with them, and they with Him. That is the great attainment," (Al-Ma'idah: 119).

Truth of the matter, we all are able to exist in all our understandings if we were to all be truthful.

Ephesians 4:25
"Therefore, having put away falsehood, let each one of you speak the truth with his neighbor, for we are members one of another."

We are members one of another!

"Those who have failed to work toward the truth have missed the purpose of living."

The I AM in me has been working on the truth since I realized that I wasn't being truthful with myself.

I had to accept the reality of things that I was doing that were harmful and weren't allowing the I AM in me to flourish. I'm free today in truth.

I am Joy! I am Peace! I am Love! I am Happiness! I am Success! I am Unstoppable!

I am Capable of going forth into this world and sharing the truth and the I AM in me will be set free.

IT IS Finished!

References

Chapter 3

"https://islam4u.pro/blog/love-in-the-quran/

Chapter 4

"Procedia - Social and Behavioral Sciences 219 (2016) 76 – 83"

https://www.pursuit-of-happiness.org/history-of-happiness/buddha/

Chapter 5

(Dhammapada 1-2 / Müller & Maguire, 2002.)

https://www.pursuit-of-happiness.org/history-of-happiness/buddha/

Chapter 8

http://buddhismnetwork.com/2016/12/08/buddha-quotes-on-truth-and-spirituality/